WoodRocket's
MW01350929
Adult Coloring Book

READY... SET...
BAKED!

TOM DANKS

FANCY A
SMOKE

UNICHRONIC

DOPERAH WINFREY

You IndiCAN Do It!

PINEANDERTHAL
EXPRESS

BUD PITT

Cowabonga

YOU'RE MY BEST BUD!

KIM KUSHDASHIAN

12
1
2
3
4
5
6
7
8
9
10
11

KEEP CALM
AND
CHEEBA ON

MORGAN JAFREEMAN

AREA 420

I'M HIGH AF

NATALIE POTMAN

LIVE LAUGH
LIGHT
ONE UP